2016 DIARY

F

FRANCES LINCOLN LIMITED

PUBLISHERS

Frances Lincoln Limited
www.franceslincoln.com

Royal Ballet Desk Diary 2016
Copyright © Frances Lincoln Limited 2015
Text and photographs copyright © Royal Opera
House unless stated otherwise.
Licensed by Royal Opera House Enterprises Ltd.

Every effort has been made to trace the
photographers of all pictures reprinted in this
diary. Acknowledgment is made in all cases where
photographer and/or source is known.

Astronomical information © Crown Copyright.
Reproduced by permission of the Controller of Her
Majesty's Stationery Office and the UK Hydrographic
Office (www.ukho.gov.uk).

A catalogue record for this book is available
from the British Library.

Designed by Arianna Osti

ISBN: 9780711236226

Printed in China

First Frances Lincoln edition 2015

9 8 7 6 5 4 3 2 1

FRONT COVER *The Winter's Tale*: choreography
Christopher Wheeldon (2014). Marianela Nuñez as
Hermione
BACK COVER Claudia Dean, Meaghan Grace
Hinkis, Gemma Pitchley-Gale and Nathalie Harrison
captured by Royal Ballet Company dancer and
photographer Andrej Uspenski.
TITLE PAGE *Electric Counterpoint*: choreography
Christopher Wheeldon (2008). Sarah Lamb
INTRODUCTION *La Bayadère*: choreography Natalia
Makarova (1989) after Marius Petipa (1877). Melissa
Hamilton as a Shade

GENERAL INFORMATION

Royal Opera House
Covent Garden
London WC2E 9DD
Switchboard: +44 (0)20 7240 1200
Box Office: +44 (0)20 7304 4000
Monday–Saturday, 10am–8pm

ROH Shop hours of opening:
Monday–Saturday, 10am–7.30pm
Telephone: +44 (0)20 7212 9331

For more information on what's on at the
Royal Opera House, please visit www.roh.org.uk.

ACKNOWLEDGMENTS

Front cover ©ROH/Johan Persson, 2014; **Back cover**
©ROH/Andrej Uspenski, 2011 **Title page** ©ROH/Johan
Persson, 2010; **Introduction** ©ROH/Tristram Kenton,
2012; **Week 1** ©ROH/Tristram Kenton, 2014; **Week
2** ©ROH/Bill Cooper, 2014; **Week 3** ©ROH/Dominik
Klimowski, 2011; **Week 4** ©ROH/Johan Persson, 2010;
Week 5 ©ROH/Dominik Klimowski, 2011; **Week 6** ©ROH/
Andrej Uspenski, 2013; **Week 7** ©ROH/Tristram Kenton
2014; **Week 8** ©ROH/Bill Cooper, 2013; **Week 9** ©ROH/
Tristram Kenton, 2012; **Week 10** ©ROH/Bill Cooper, 2012;
Week 11 ©Frederika Davis, 1965; **Week 12** ©ROH/Johan
Persson, 2011; **Week 13** ©ROH/Tristram Kenton, 2014;
Week 14 ©ROH/Johan Persson, 2014; **Week 15** ©ROH/
Roger Wood, 1949; **Week 16** ©ROH/Tristram Kenton, 2013;
Week 17 ©ROH/Roger Wood, 1948; **Week 18** ©ROH/Andrej
Uspenski, 2013; **Week 19** ©ROH, 1987; **Week 20** ©ROH/
Bill Cooper, 2011; **Week 21** ©Frederika Davis, 1964; **Week
22** ©ROH/Johan Persson, 2014; **Week 23** ©Sim Cannetty-
Clarke, 2007; **Week 24** ©ROH/Johan Persson, 2014; **Week
25** ©ROH/Bill Cooper, 2011; **Week 26** ©ROH/Tristram
Kenton, 2013; **Week 27** ©ROH/Tristram Kenton, 2012; **Week
28** ©ROH/Bill Cooper, 2013; **Week 29** ©ROH/Tristram
Kenton, 2014; **Week 30** ©ROH/Johan Persson, 2012; **Week
31** ©ROH/Tristram Kenton, 2013; **Week 32** ©ROH/Johan
Persson, 2010; **Week 33** ©ROH/Tristram Kenton, 2012;
Week 34 ©ROH/Tristram Kenton, 2013; **Week 35** ©ROH/
Bill Cooper 2014; **Week 36** ©ROH/Johan Persson 2013;
Week 37 ©Frederika Davis, 1970; **Week 38** ©ROH/Tristram
Kenton, 2013; **Week 39** ©ROH/Johan Persson, 2014; **Week
40** ©Frederika Davis, 1963; **Week 41** ©ROH/Bill Cooper,
2014; **Week 42** ©ROH/Bill Cooper, 2010; **Week 43** ©ROH/
Tristram Kenton, 2012; **Week 44** ©ROH/Johan Persson,
2014; **Week 45** ©ROH/Johan Persson, 2014; **Week 46**
©ROH/Bill Cooper, 2011; **Week 47** ©ROH, 2008; **Week 48**
©David Walker, 1977; **Week 49** ©ROH/Johan Persson, 2014;
Week 50 ©ROH/Johan Persson, 2013; **Week 51** ©ROH/
Andrej Uspenski, 2011; **Week 52** ©ROH/Johan Persson,
2014; **Week 53** ©ROH/Bill Cooper, 2013

CALENDAR 2016

JANUARY

M	T	W	T	F	S	S
				1	2	3
4	5	6	7	8	9	10
11	12	13	14	15	16	17
18	19	20	21	22	23	24
25	26	27	28	29	30	31

FEBRUARY

M	T	W	T	F	S	S
1	2	3	4	5	6	7
8	9	10	11	12	13	14
15	16	17	18	19	20	21
22	23	24	25	26	27	28
29						

MARCH

M	T	W	T	F	S	S
	1	2	3	4	5	6
7	8	9	10	11	12	13
14	15	16	17	18	19	20
21	22	23	24	25	26	27
28	29	30	31			

APRIL

M	T	W	T	F	S	S
				1	2	3
4	5	6	7	8	9	10
11	12	13	14	15	16	17
18	19	20	21	22	23	24
25	26	27	28	29	30	

MAY

M	T	W	T	F	S	S
						1
2	3	4	5	6	7	8
9	10	11	12	13	14	15
16	17	18	19	20	21	22
23	24	25	26	27	28	29
30	31					

JUNE

M	T	W	T	F	S	S
		1	2	3	4	5
6	7	8	9	10	11	12
13	14	15	16	17	18	19
20	21	22	23	24	25	26
27	28	29	30			

JULY

M	T	W	T	F	S	S
				1	2	3
4	5	6	7	8	9	10
11	12	13	14	15	16	17
18	19	20	21	22	23	24
25	26	27	28	29	30	31

AUGUST

M	T	W	T	F	S	S
1	2	3	4	5	6	7
8	9	10	11	12	13	14
15	16	17	18	19	20	21
22	23	24	25	26	27	28
29	30	31				

SEPTEMBER

M	T	W	T	F	S	S
			1	2	3	4
5	6	7	8	9	10	11
12	13	14	15	16	17	18
19	20	21	22	23	24	25
26	27	28	29	30		

OCTOBER

M	T	W	T	F	S	S
					1	2
3	4	5	6	7	8	9
10	11	12	13	14	15	16
17	18	19	20	21	22	23
24	25	26	27	28	29	30
31						

NOVEMBER

M	T	W	T	F	S	S
	1	2	3	4	5	6
7	8	9	10	11	12	13
14	15	16	17	18	19	20
21	22	23	24	25	26	27
28	29	30				

DECEMBER

M	T	W	T	F	S	S
			1	2	3	4
5	6	7	8	9	10	11
12	13	14	15	16	17	18
19	20	21	22	23	24	25
26	27	28	29	30	31	

CALENDAR 2017

JANUARY

M	T	W	T	F	S	S
						1
2	3	4	5	6	7	8
9	10	11	12	13	14	15
16	17	18	19	20	21	22
23	24	25	26	27	28	29
30	31					

FEBRUARY

M	T	W	T	F	S	S
		1	2	3	4	5
6	7	8	9	10	11	12
13	14	15	16	17	18	19
20	21	22	23	24	25	26
27	28					

MARCH

M	T	W	T	F	S	S
		1	2	3	4	5
6	7	8	9	10	11	12
13	14	15	16	17	18	19
20	21	22	23	24	25	26
27	28	29	30	31		

APRIL

M	T	W	T	F	S	S
					1	2
3	4	5	6	7	8	9
10	11	12	13	14	15	16
17	18	19	20	21	22	23
24	25	26	27	28	29	30

MAY

M	T	W	T	F	S	S
1	2	3	4	5	6	7
8	9	10	11	12	13	14
15	16	17	18	19	20	21
22	23	24	25	26	27	28
29	30	31				

JUNE

M	T	W	T	F	S	S
			1	2	3	4
5	6	7	8	9	10	11
12	13	14	15	16	17	18
19	20	21	22	23	24	25
26	27	28	29	30		

JULY

M	T	W	T	F	S	S
					1	2
3	4	5	6	7	8	9
10	11	12	13	14	15	16
17	18	19	20	21	22	23
24	25	26	27	28	29	30
31						

AUGUST

M	T	W	T	F	S	S
	1	2	3	4	5	6
7	8	9	10	11	12	13
14	15	16	17	18	19	20
21	22	23	24	25	26	27
28	29	30	31			

SEPTEMBER

M	T	W	T	F	S	S
				1	2	3
4	5	6	7	8	9	10
11	12	13	14	15	16	17
18	19	20	21	22	23	24
25	26	27	28	29	30	

OCTOBER

M	T	W	T	F	S	S
						1
2	3	4	5	6	7	8
9	10	11	12	13	14	15
16	17	18	19	20	21	22
23	24	25	26	27	28	29
30	31					

NOVEMBER

M	T	W	T	F	S	S
		1	2	3	4	5
6	7	8	9	10	11	12
13	14	15	16	17	18	19
20	21	22	23	24	25	26
27	28	29	30			

DECEMBER

M	T	W	T	F	S	S
				1	2	3
4	5	6	7	8	9	10
11	12	13	14	15	16	17
18	19	20	21	22	23	24
25	26	27	28	29	30	31

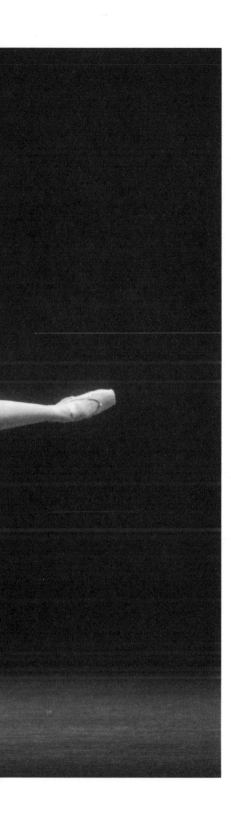

ROYAL BALLET

Patron **HM The Queen**
President **HRH The Prince of Wales**
Vice-President **The Lady Sarah Chatto**

Director **Kevin O'Hare**
Music Director **Koen Kessels**

Resident Choreographer
Wayne McGregor CBE
Artistic Associate
Christopher Wheeldon

INTRODUCTION

The Royal Ballet is one of the most famous ballet companies in the world and internationally renowned for its artistic and creative excellence. It was founded by Dame Ninette de Valois in 1931 as Vic-Wells Ballet and was given a long-term base at Sadler's Wells Theatre. During World War II the Company, by now called Sadler's Wells Ballet, toured the UK and Europe performing for Allied Troops. In 1946, it transferred to its new home at the Royal Opera House in Covent Garden. For the Company's 25th anniversary in 1956, it was granted a Royal Charter, becoming The Royal Ballet. (Its touring arm, the Theatre Ballet, eventually returned to Sadler's Wells, later becoming Sadler's Wells Royal Ballet, now independent as Birmingham Royal Ballet.)

The Royal Ballet maintains a vast repertory comprising the great classics and heritage works by its two great 20th-century choreographers, Founder Choreographer Frederick Ashton and Kenneth MacMillan, and others including John Cranko, George Balanchine and Jerome Robbins. It continues to foster new work from today's foremost choreographers and most exciting young dance-makers.

In its history The Royal Ballet has nurtured some of the world's greatest dancers, including Moira Shearer, Margot Fonteyn (the Company's Prima Ballerina Assoluta), Rudolf Nureyev, Antoinette Sibley, Anthony Dowell, Darcey Bussell and Carlos Acosta. The Company also performs its wide-ranging repertory on tour, and reaches a far wider audience through live cinema broadcasts worldwide. Among its current Principal roster are some of the finest dancers in the world today.

DECEMBER & JANUARY

28 Monday

Holiday, UK, Republic of Ireland, Canada, Australia and New Zealand

---

29 Tuesday

---

30 Wednesday

---

31 Thursday

New Year's Eve

---

1 Friday

Holiday, UK, Republic of Ireland, USA, Canada, Australia and New Zealand

---

2 Saturday

Last Quarter
Holiday, Scotland and New Zealand

---

3 Sunday

The Sleeping Beauty: choreography Marius Petipa (1890). Vadim Muntagirov as Prince Florimund and Akane Takada as Princess Aurora (2006 production)

JANUARY

4 Monday

5 Tuesday

6 Wednesday   Epiphany

7 Thursday

8 Friday

9 Saturday

10 Sunday   *New Moon*

The Dream: choreography Frederick Ashton (1964). Steven McRae as Oberon

JANUARY

11 Monday

12 Tuesday

13 Wednesday

14 Thursday

15 Friday

16 Saturday   *First Quarter*

17 Sunday

Shoes worn by the French Suitor in the 2006 production of *The Sleeping Beauty*

JANUARY

18 Monday   Holiday, USA (Martin Luther King Jnr Day)

19 Tuesday

20 Wednesday

21 Thursday

22 Friday

23 Saturday

24 Sunday   *Full Moon*

Electric Counterpoint: choreography Christopher Wheeldon (2008): Marianela Nuñez

JANUARY

25 Monday

26 Tuesday   Holiday, Australia (Australia Day)

27 Wednesday

28 Thursday

29 Friday

30 Saturday

31 Sunday

Front of house at the Royal Opera House

FEBRUARY

1 Monday *Last Quarter*

2 Tuesday

3 Wednesday

4 Thursday

5 Friday

6 Saturday
Accession of Queen Elizabeth II
Holiday, New Zealand (Waitangi Day)

7 Sunday

Artists of The Royal Ballet captured by Royal Ballet Company dancer and photographer Andrej Uspenski

FEBRUARY

---

8 Monday

---

9 Tuesday

Shrove Tuesday

---

10 Wednesday

Ash Wednesday

---

11 Thursday

---

12 Friday

---

13 Saturday

---

14 Sunday

Valentine's Day

The Sleeping Beauty: choreography Marius Petipa (1890). Lauren Cuthbertson as Princess Aurora and Matthew Golding as Prince Florimund (2006 production)

FEBRUARY

15 Monday

First Quarter
Holiday, USA (Presidents' Day)

16 Tuesday

17 Wednesday

18 Thursday

19 Friday

20 Saturday

21 Sunday

'Rubies' *(Jewels)*: choreography George Balanchine (1967). Natalia Osipova (2007 production)

FEBRUARY

22 Monday   *Full Moon*

23 Tuesday

24 Wednesday

25 Thursday

26 Friday

27 Saturday

28 Sunday

Marguerite and Armand: choreography Frederick Ashton (1963). Zenaida Yanowsky as Marguerite and Federico Bonelli as Armand

29 Monday

1 Tuesday

Last Quarter
St. David's Day

2 Wednesday

3 Thursday

4 Friday

5 Saturday

6 Sunday

Mother's Day, UK and Republic of Ireland

Sweet Violets: choreography Liam Scarlett (2012). Emma Maguire as Little Dot

MARCH

7 Monday

8 Tuesday

9 Wednesday   *New Moon*

10 Thursday

11 Friday

12 Saturday

13 Sunday

Romeo and Juliet: choreography Kenneth MacMillan (1965). Rudolf Nureyev as Romeo and Margot Fonteyn as Juliet

MARCH

---

14 Monday   Commonwealth Day

---

15 Tuesday   *First Quarter*

---

16 Wednesday

---

17 Thursday   St. Patrick's Day

---

18 Friday

---

19 Saturday

---

20 Sunday   Palm Sunday

Manon: choreography Kenneth MacMillan (1974). Thiago Soares as Lescaut

MARCH

21 Monday

22 Tuesday

23 Wednesday   *Full Moon*

24 Thursday   Maundy Thursday

25 Friday   Good Friday
Holiday, UK, Canada, Australia and New Zealand

26 Saturday   Holiday Australia (Easter Saturday)

27 Sunday   Easter Sunday
British Summer Time begins

The Sleeping Beauty: choreography Marius Petipa (1890). Tristan Dyer, Yasmine Naghdi and Beatriz Stix-Brunell as Florestan and his sisters (2006 production)

28 Monday

29 Tuesday

30 Wednesday

31 Thursday

Last Quarter

1 Friday

2 Saturday

3 Sunday

Gloria: choreography Kenneth MacMillan (1980). Melissa Hamilton

APRIL

4 Monday

5 Tuesday

6 Wednesday

7 Thursday   *New Moon*

8 Friday

9 Saturday

10 Sunday

In costume for *Cinderella*, choreography Frederick Ashton (1948). Pauline Wadsworth, Dorothea Zaymes and Jean Stokes, Sadler's Wells Theatre Ballet

APRIL

11 Monday

12 Tuesday

13 Wednesday

14 Thursday   *Quarter*

15 Friday

16 Saturday

17 Sunday

Voices of Spring: choreography Frederick Ashton (1981). Yuhui Choe

APRIL

18 Monday

19 Tuesday

20 Wednesday

21 Thursday   Birthday of Queen Elizabeth II

22 Friday   *Full Moon*

23 Saturday   St George's Day
First day of Passover (Pesach)

24 Sunday

Cinderella: choreography Frederick Ashton (1948). Moira Shearer as Cinderella, Sadler's Wells
Theatre Ballet

APRIL & MAY

25 Monday

Anzac Day
Holiday, Australia and New Zealand

26 Tuesday

27 Wednesday

28 Thursday

29 Friday

30 Saturday

Last Quarter

1 Sunday

Taking a curtain call for *Swan Lake*, choreography Marius Petipa and Lev Ivanov (1895). Marianela Nuñez as Odile and Thiago Soares as Prince Siegfried (1987 production)

2 Monday

Early Spring Bank Holiday
UK and Republic of Ireland

3 Tuesday

4 Wednesday

5 Thursday

Ascension Day

6 Friday

New Moon

7 Saturday

8 Sunday

Mother's Day, USA and Canada

Tutu designed by Yolanda Sonnabend for the 1987 production of *Swan Lake*

MAY

9 Monday

10 Tuesday

11 Wednesday

12 Thursday

13 Friday   *First Quarter*

14 Saturday

15 Sunday   Whit Sunday

Live Fire Exercise: choreography Wayne McGregor (2011). Akane Takada

16 Monday

---

17 Tuesday

---

18 Wednesday

---

19 Thursday

---

20 Friday

---

21 Saturday   *Full Moon*

---

22 Sunday   Trinity Sunday

The Dream: choreography Frederick Ashton (1964). Antoinette Sibley as Titania and Anthony Dowell as Oberon

MAY

23 Monday   Victoria Day Holiday, Canada

24 Tuesday

25 Wednesday

26 Thursday   Corpus Christi

27 Friday

28 Saturday

29 Sunday   *Last Quarter*

The Winter's Tale: choreography Christopher Wheeldon (2014). Lauren Cuthbertson as Hermione

30 Monday   Spring Bank Holiday, UK and Republic of Ireland

31 Tuesday

1 Wednesday

2 Thursday   Coronation Day

3 Friday

4 Saturday

5 Sunday   *New Moon*

The shoe room at the Royal Opera House

JUNE

6 Monday

7

First day of Ramadan
(subject to sighting of the moon)

8 Wednesday

9 Thursday

10 Friday

11 Saturday

The Queen's Official Birthday
(Date subject to confirmation)

12 Sunday

First Quarter
Feast of Weeks (Shavuot)

The Winter's Tale: choreography Christopher Wheeldon (2014). Steven McRae as Florizel and Federico Bonelli as Polixenes

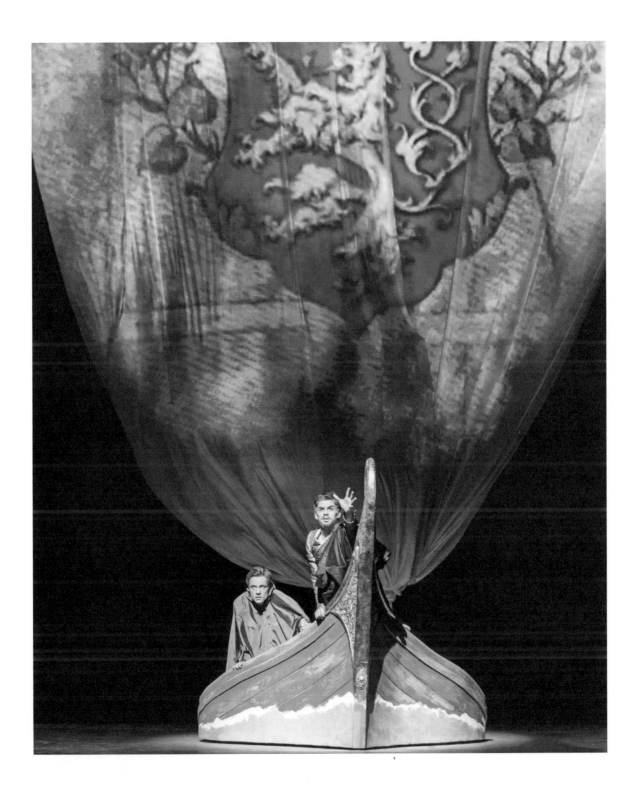

13 Monday

14 Tuesday

15 Wednesday

16 Thursday

17 Friday

18 Saturday

19 Sunday

Father's Day
UK, Republic of Ireland, USA and Canada

Enigma Variations: choreography Frederick Ashton (1968). Christina Arestis as Lady Elgar

JUNE

20 Monday

Full Moon
Summer Solstice (Summer begins)

21 Tuesday

22 Wednesday

23 Thursday

24 Friday

25 Saturday

26 Sunday

La Bayadère: choreography Natalia Makarova (1989) after Marius Petipa (1877). Roberta Marquez as Nikiya and Steven McRae as Solor

27 Monday   *Last Quarter*

---

28 Tuesday

---

29 Wednesday

---

30 Thursday

---

1 Friday   Holiday, Canada (Canada Day)

---

2 Saturday

---

3 Sunday

The Firebird: choreography Mikhail Fokine (1910). Itziar Mendizabal as the Firebird (1954 production)

JULY

4 Monday

New Moon
Independence Day, USA

5 Tuesday

Eid al-Fitr (end of Ramadan)
(subject to sighting of the moon)

6 Wednesday

7 Thursday

8 Friday

9 Saturday

10 Sunday

Romeo and Juliet: choreography Kenneth MacMillan (1965). Natalia Osipova as Juliet

JULY

---

11 Monday

---

12 Tuesday

First Quarter
Holiday, Northern Ireland (Battle of the Boyne)

---

13 Wednesday

---

14 Thursday

---

15 Friday

St. Swithin's Day

---

16 Saturday

---

17 Sunday

Five Brahms Waltzes in the Manner of Isadora Duncan: choreography Frederick Ashton (1976).
Romany Pajdak

JULY

18 Monday

19 Tuesday   *Full Moon*

20 Wednesday

21 Thursday

22 Friday

23 Saturday

24 Sunday

The Prince of the Pagodas: choreography Kenneth MacMillan (1989). Nehemiah Kish as the Prince, Alexander Campbell as the Fool and Steven McRae as King of the West

25 Monday

26 Tuesday   *Last Quarter*

27 Wednesday

28 Thursday

29 Friday

30 Saturday

31 Sunday

La Valse: choreography Frederick Ashton (1959). Ryoichi Hirano and Hikaru Kobayashi

AUGUST

1 Monday   Holiday, Scotland and Republic of Ireland

2 Tuesday   *New Moon*

3 Wednesday

4 Thursday

5 Friday

6 Saturday

7 Sunday

Electric Counterpoint: choreography Christopher Wheeldon (2008). Eric Underwood

AUGUST

8 Monday

9 Tuesday

10 Wednesday   *First Quarter*

11 Thursday

12 Friday

13 Saturday

14 Sunday

In the Night: choreography Jerome Robbins (1970). Zenaida Yanowsky and Nehemiah Kish (1973 production)

AUGUST

15 Monday

16 Tuesday

17 Wednesday

18 Thursday   *Full Moon*

19 Friday

20 Saturday

21 Sunday

La Bayadère: choreography Natalia Makarova (1989) after Marius Petipa (1877). Laura Morera as Gamzatti

AUGUST

22 Monday

23 Tuesday

24 Wednesday

25 Thursday   *Last Quarter*

26 Friday

27 Saturday

28 Sunday

Connectome: choreography Alastair Marriott (2014). Marcelino Sambé

AUGUST & SEPTEMBER

29 Monday   Holiday, UK (exc. Scotland)

30 Tuesday

31 Wednesday

1 Thursday   *New Moon*

2 Friday

3 Saturday

4 Sunday   Father's Day, Australia and New Zealand

Apollo: choreography George Balanchine (1928). Sarah Lamb as Terpsichore and Rupert Pennefather as Apollo (1966 production)

SEPTEMBER

5 Monday

Holiday, Canada (Labour Day)
Holiday, USA (Labor Day)

6 Tuesday

7 Wednesday

8 Thursday

9 Friday

First Quarter

10 Saturday

11 Sunday

The Ropes of Time: choreography Rudi van Dantzig (1970). Rudolf Nureyev as the Traveller

SEPTEMBER

12 Monday

13 Tuesday

14 Wednesday

15 Thursday

16 Friday   *Full Moon*

17 Saturday

18 Sunday

The Nutcracker: choreography Peter Wright (1984) after Lev Ivanov and Marius Petipa (1892). Francesca Hayward as Clara

SEPTEMBER

---

19 Monday

---

20 Tuesday

---

21 Wednesday

---

22 Thursday   Autumnal Equinox (Autumn begins)

---

23 Friday   *Last Quarter*

---

24 Saturday

---

25 Sunday

The Winter's Tale: choreography Christopher Wheeldon (2014). Zenaida Yanowsky as Paulina

SEPTEMBER & OCTOBER

26 Monday

27 Tuesday

28 Wednesday

29 Thursday   Michaelmas Day

30 Friday

1 Saturday   *New Moon*

2 Sunday

Swan Lake: choreography Marius Petipa and Lev Ivanov (1895): Margot Fonteyn as Odette (1963 production)

OCTOBER

3 Monday

Jewish New Year (Rosh Hashanah)
and Islamic New Year

4 Tuesday

5 Wednesday

6 Thursday

7 Friday

8 Saturday

9 Sunday

First Quarter

The Sleeping Beauty: choreography Marius Petipa (1890). Lauren Cuthbertson as Princess Aurora (2006 production)

OCTOBER

10 Monday

11 Tuesday

12 Wednesday   Day of Atonement (Yom Kippur)

13 Thursday

14 Friday

15 Saturday

16 Sunday   *Full Moon*

Onegin: choreography John Cranko (1965). Laura Morera as Tatiana and Federico Bonelli as Eugene Onegin

OCTOBER

17 Monday   First day of Tabernacles (Sukkot)

18 Tuesday

19 Wednesday

20 Thursday

21 Friday

22 Saturday   *Last Quarter*

23 Sunday

Giselle: choreography Marius Petipa after Jules Perrot and Jean Coralli (1884). Roberta Marquez as Giselle (1985 production)

OCTOBER

24 Monday

Holiday, New Zealand (Labour Day)

25 Tuesday

26 Wednesday

27 Thursday

28 Friday

29 Saturday

30 Sunday

New Moon
British Summer Time ends

The Winter's Tale: choreography Christopher Wheeldon (2014). Edward Watson as Leontes

OCTOBER & NOVEMBER

31 Monday   Halloween

---

1 Tuesday   All Saints' Day

---

2 Wednesday

---

3 Thursday

---

4 Friday

---

5 Saturday   Guy Fawkes

---

6 Sunday

The Winter's Tale: choreography Christopher Wheeldon (2014). Lauren Cuthbertson as Hermione and Edward Watson as Leontes

NOVEMBER

7 Monday   *First Quarter*

8 Tuesday

9 Wednesday

10 Thursday

11 Friday   Holiday, USA (Veterans' Day) and Canada (Remembrance Day)

12 Saturday

13 Sunday   Remembrance Sunday

Swan Lake: choreography Marius Petipa and Lev Ivanov (1895). Roberta Marquez as Odette (1987 production)

NOVEMBER

14 Monday   *Full Moon*

15 Tuesday

16 Wednesday

17 Thursday

18 Friday

19 Saturday

20 Sunday

Tutu designed by Jean-Denis Malclès for the 1948 production of *Cinderella*

NOVEMBER

21 Monday   *Last Quarter*

---

22 Tuesday

---

23 Wednesday

---

24 Thursday   Holiday, USA (Thanksgiving)

---

25 Friday

---

26 Saturday

---

27 Sunday   First Sunday in Advent

Costume design for the 1977 production of *The Sleeping Beauty*

Royal Opera House, Covent Garden, The Sleeping Beauty.
Fairy of the Eenchanted Garden (second version)

David Walker
1977

28 Monday

29 Tuesday   *New Moon*

30 Wednesday   St. Andrew's Day

1 Thursday

2 Friday

3 Saturday

4 Sunday

Don Quixote: choreography Carlos Acosta (2013) after Marius Petipa (1873). Ryoichi Hirano as Espada and Laura Morera as Mercedes

DECEMBER

5 Monday

6 Tuesday

7 Wednesday   *First Quarter*

8 Thursday

9 Friday

10 Saturday

11 Sunday

Raven Girl: choreography Wayne McGregor (2013). Sarah Lamb as Raven Girl

DECEMBER

12 Monday

13 Tuesday

14 Wednesday   *Full Moon*

15 Thursday

16 Friday

17 Saturday

18 Sunday

Claudia Dean, Meaghan Grace Hinkis, Gemma Pitchley-Gale and Nathalie Harrison captured by Royal Ballet Company dancer and photographer Andrej Uspenski

DECEMBER

19 Monday

20 Tuesday   Winter Solstice (Winter begins)

21 Wednesday   *Last Quarter*

22 Thursday

23 Friday

24 Saturday   Christmas Eve
                                                                        Hannukah begins

25 Sunday   Christmas Day

The Winter's Tale: choreography Christopher Wheeldon (2014). Steven McRae as Florizel

DECEMBER & JANUARY 2017

26 Monday
Holiday, UK, Republic of Ireland, Canada, Australia and New Zealand
Boxing Day (St. Stephen's Day)

27 Tuesday
Holiday, UK, Republic of Ireland, USA, Canada,
Australia and New Zealand

28 Wednesday

29 Thursday
New Moon

30 Friday

31 Saturday
New Year's Eve

1 Sunday
New Year's Day
Holiday, UK, Republic of Ireland, USA, Canada, Australia and
New Zealand

'Diamonds' (*Jewels*): choreography George Balanchine (1967). Marianela Nuñez (2007 production)

NOTES